TRAIN *your* BRAIN

PUZZLE BOOK

Brain-Bending Challenges—Intermediate

First edition for the United States, its territories and dependencies, and Canada published in 2014 by Barron's Educational Series, Inc.

Text and puzzle content copyright © British Mensa Limited 1994 & 1997 & 2010
Design and artwork copyright © Carlton Books Limited 1994 & 1997 & 2010 & 2014

Originally published in 2014 as *Train Your Brain Puzzle Book Level 2 for Confident Puzzlers* by Carlton Books Limited
An imprint of the Carlton Publishing Group
20 Mortimer Street, London, W1T 3JW

Senior Editor: Alexandra Koken
Designed by: Katie Baxendale
Production: Marion Storz

U.S. edition copyright © 2014 by Barron's Educational Series, Inc.

All inquiries should be addressed to:
Barron's Educational Series, Inc.
250 Wireless Boulevard
Hauppauge, New York 11788
www.barronseduc.com

ISBN: 978-1-4380-0538-6

Library of Congress Control Number: 2014930894

Date of Manufacture: July 2014
Manufactured by: RR Donnelley South China, Dongguan, China

Printed in China
9 8 7 6 5 4 3 2 1

TRAIN your BRAIN

PUZZLE BOOK

Brain-Bending Challenges

INTERMEDIATE

BARRON'S

INTRODUCTION

SO YOU THINK YOUR BRAIN IS BUZZING?

PROVE IT WITH THIS LITTLE BOOK OF TRICKY PUZZLES!

TRAIN YOUR BRAIN

is packed with questions to test your verbal and numerical reasoning. To solve them you'll need the ability to think logically, plus some staying power when the problems get tough.

BRAIN-BENDING CHALLENGES is the second book in the *Train Your Brain* series: check out **MIND-TWISTING PUZZLES** for easier puzzles and **SUPER TRICKY TEASERS** for the real toughies.

Now, put on your thinking cap, turn the page, and let the training begin!

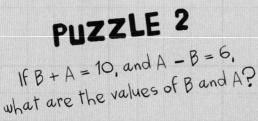

UP AND AT 'EM!

PUZZLE 1

What is two-thirds of one-third? Is it one-third, one quarter, or two-ninths?

PUZZLE 2

If B + A = 10, and A − B = 6, what are the values of B and A?

PUZZLE 3

Move up or across from the bottom
left-hand 3 to the top right-hand 3.
Collect nine numbers and add them together.
What is the lowest you can score?

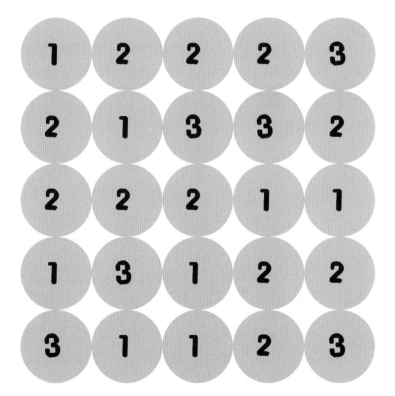

PUZZLE 4

The symbols in the grid on the opposite page have been drawn in a certain sequence, starting top left. When you have figured out what it is, you should be able to decide which of the boxes below would correctly fit in the blank space.

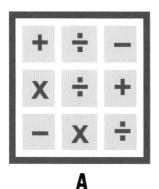

A

B

C

D

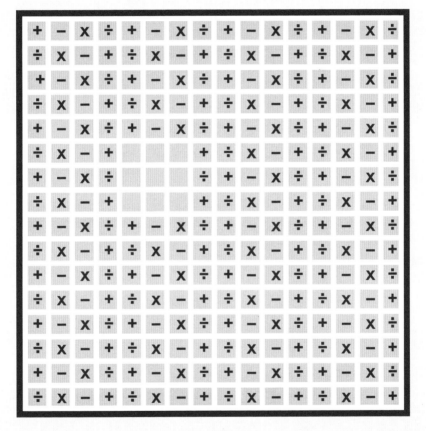

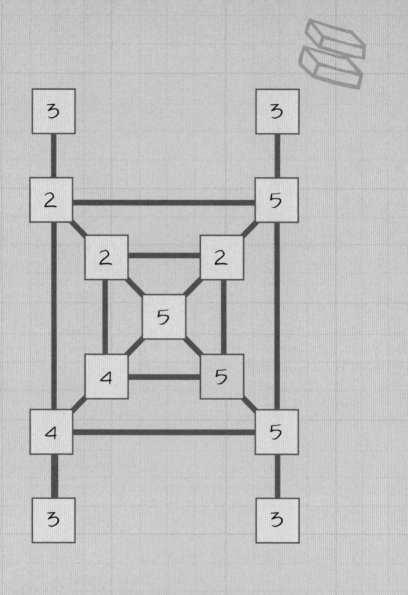

PUZZLE 5

Start at any corner and follow the lines. Add up the first four numbers you meet and then add on the corner number. What is the highest you can score?

PUZZLE 6

Place in the middle box a number larger than 1. If the number is the correct one, all the other numbers can be divided by it without leaving any remainder. What is the number?

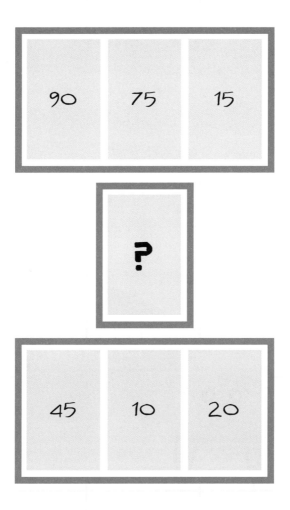

PUZZLE 7

If two apples are needed to make an apple cake, and there are four apples to a pound, how many cakes can be made from 5 pounds of apples?

LIMBERING UP!

Circle sectors with numbers: 3, 2, 7, 2, 2, 4, 9, 2, 8, 2, 1, 6, 2, 1, 6, ?, 5, 4, 5, 3, 4, 5, 3, 4, 4, 5, 3, 6

PUZZLE 8

Each sector of the circle follows a pattern. What number should replace the question mark?

PUZZLE 9

At a birthday party half the guests drink cola, a quarter have lemonade, a sixth have orange juice, and the remaining three have water. How many guests were at the party?

PUZZLE 10

Cut out these shapes carefully
and rearrange them to form a
number. What is it?

PUZZLE 11

Can you unravel the logic of these squares and find the missing number?

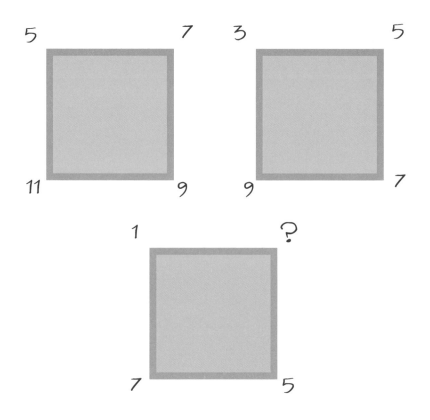

5   7   3   5

11   9   9   7

            1   ?

            7   5

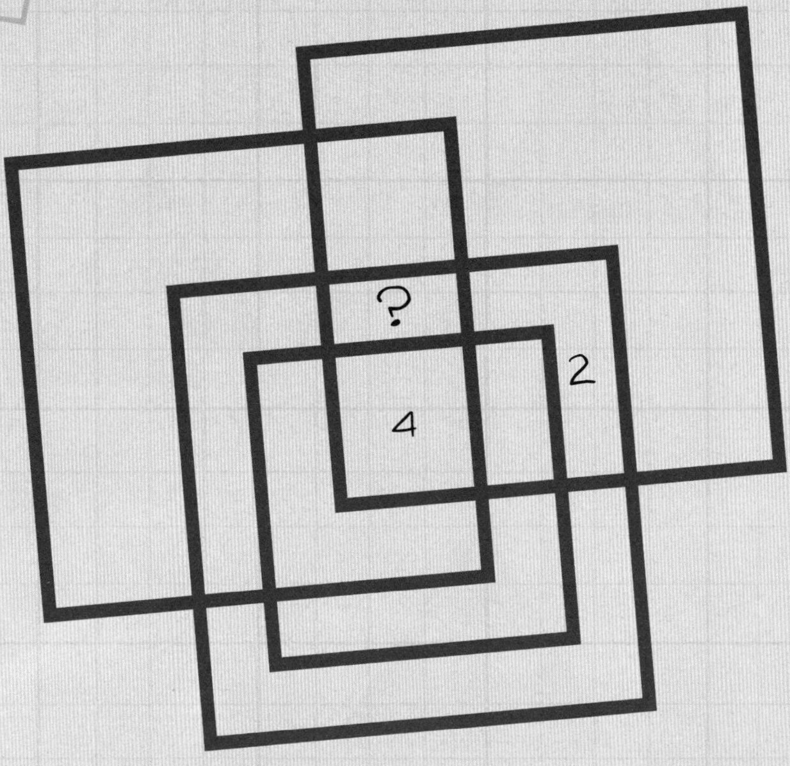

?

2

4

PUZZLE 12

If you look carefully you should see why the numbers are written as they are. What number should replace the question mark?

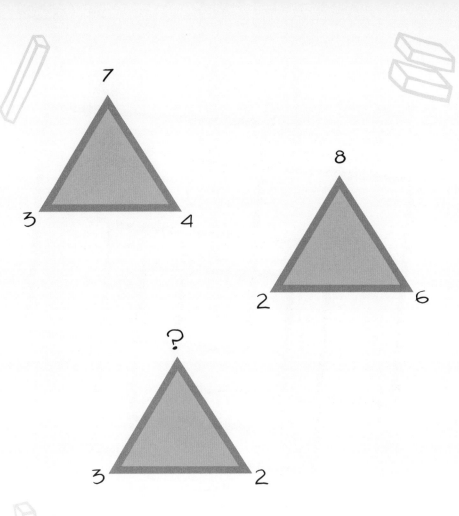

PUZZLE 13

These triangles have been numbered using a certain logic. When you have figured out what it is you will discover what number replaces the question mark.

PUZZLE 14

Each slice of this cake adds up to the same number. All the numbers going around the cake total 32. Which numbers should appear in the blanks?

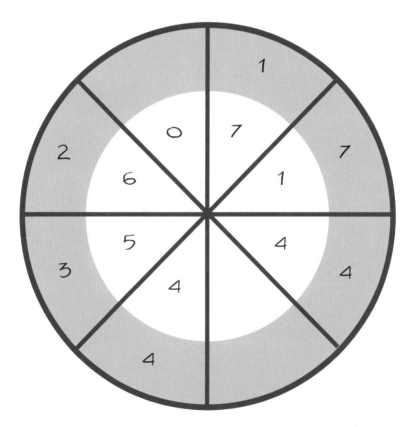

PUZZLE 15

This may look just like a puzzle you have seen elsewhere in this book, but this time the logic is different! What number replaces the question mark?

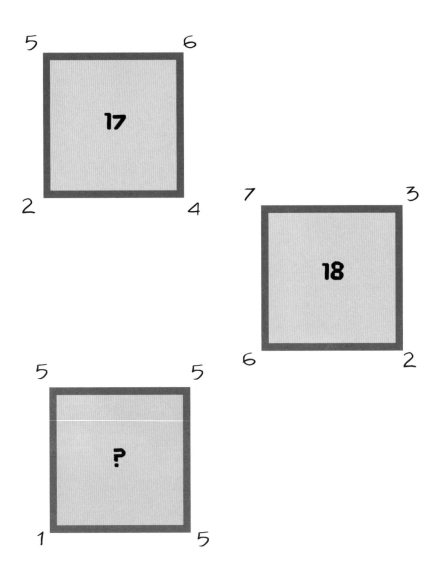

F	4E	1S	6S	2W	6S
5S	1N	1E	2E	4W	2S
4E	1W	3E	2N	4S	2W
2E	1W	1S	2S	3W	2S
1E	3N	2N	2E	1N	1W
1N	3N	2E	1N	5N	5W
6N	1N	1N	1W	5N	4W

PUZZLE 16

Here is an unusual safe. Each of the buttons must be pressed only once in the correct order to open it. The last button is marked F. The number of moves and the direction is marked on each button. Thus 1N would mean one move north, while 1W would mean one move to the west. Which button is the first you must press? Here's a clue: it can be found in the middle row.

PUZZLE 17

If you write the alphabet in a circle, which letter would be nine places backward from F? Is it X, W, or T?

PUZZLE 18

A boy rides his bicycle at 12 miles per hour. How many minutes will it take him to reach the next village, 9 miles from his house?

Z

PUZZLE 19

Look at each line of numbers in the diagram. What number should replace the question mark?

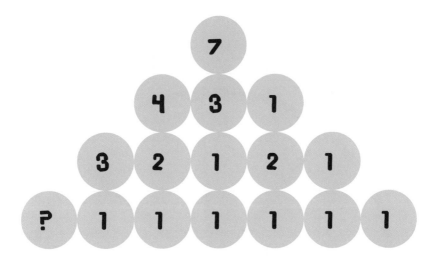

PUZZLE 20

Can you replace the question mark
with a number in this circle?

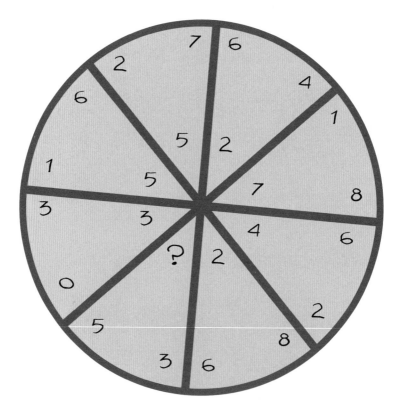

1V **2V** **10V** **5V**

20V **50V**

PUZZLE 21

On the planet Venox the coins used are 1V, 2V, 5V, 10V, 20V, and 50V. A Venoxian has 306V in his squiggly bank. He has the same number of four kinds of coin. How many of each are there and what are they?

PUZZLE 22

If A = 13, B = 3A, and C = A + B,
what is the value of C?

PUZZLE 23

Start at the A and move to B, passing through various parts of the horse. There is a number in each part and these must be added together. What is the lowest total you can find?

PUZZLE 24

Which numbers will the hands of the
fourth clock, below, point to?

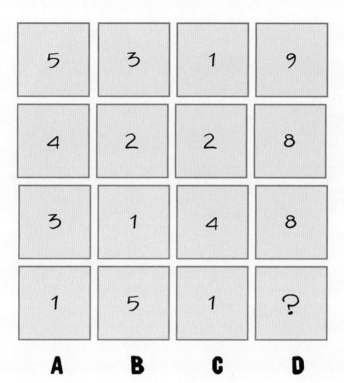

A	B	C	D
5	3	1	9
4	2	2	8
3	1	4	8
1	5	1	?

PUZZLE 25

The numbers in column D are linked in some way to those in A, B, and C. What number replaces the question mark?

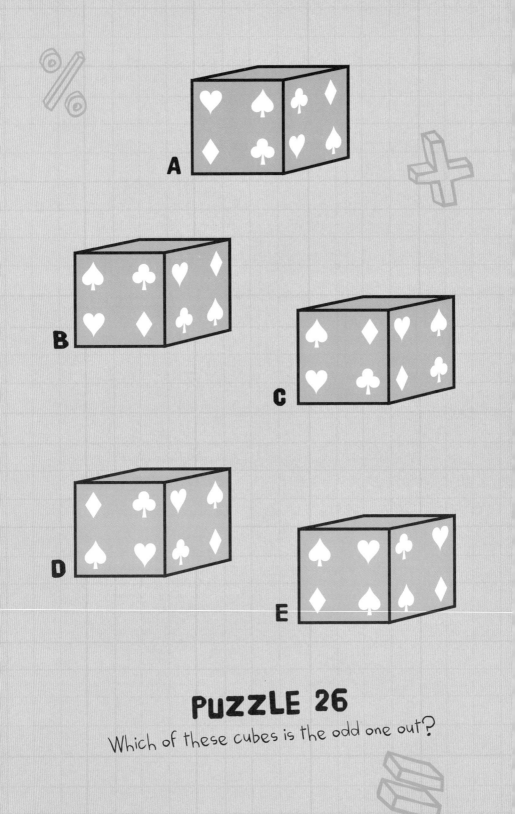

PUZZLE 26

Which of these cubes is the odd one out?

PUZZLE 27

Move from the bottom left-hand 4 to the top right-hand 3, adding together all five numbers. Each blue circle is worth negative 1, and this should be taken away from your total each time you meet one. What is the highest total you can find?

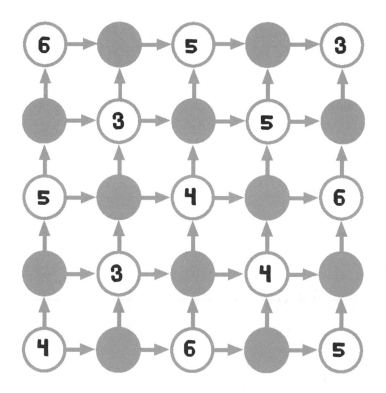

PUZZLE 28

What number comes next in this series, replacing the question mark?

12	21	36	63	45	?

THIS IS A
TRICKY ONE!

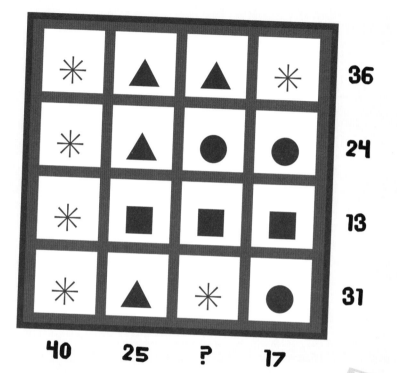

36

24

13

31

40   **25**   **?**   **17**

PUZZLE 29

Each symbol is worth a number. The total of the symbols can be found alongside each row and column. What number should replace the question mark?

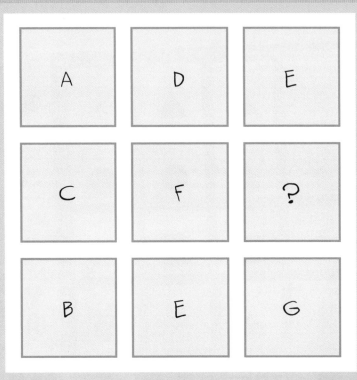

A	D	E
C	F	?
B	E	G

PUZZLE 30

Which letter is needed to complete the diagram below? Is it K, G, or I?

PUZZLE 31

What is the lowest number of straight lines needed to divide the rhinoceros so that you can find the numbers 1, 2, 3, 4, and 5 in each section?

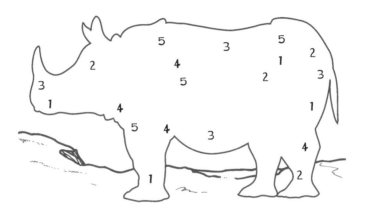

PUZZLE 32

Replace each question mark with plus, minus, multiply, or divide. Each sign can be used more than once. When the correct ones have been used, the sum will be completed. What are the signs?

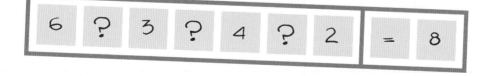

6 ? 3 ? 4 ? 2 = 8

PUZZLE 33

Choose a letter to replace the
question mark. Is it A, R, or Q?

PUZZLE 34

Follow the arrows and find the longest possible route. How many boxes have been entered?

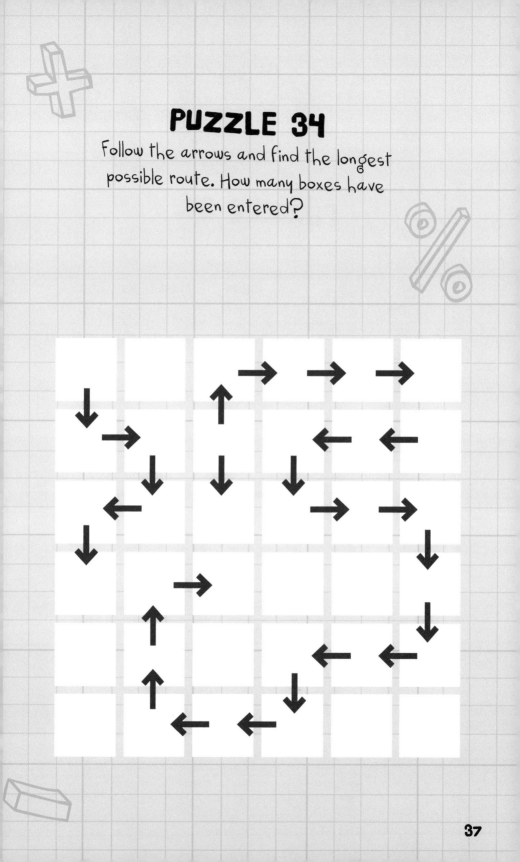

PUZZLE 35

Which square of nine letters should replace the one that's missing? The first letter is A at the top left corner, and the series runs in a diagonal zigzag with the order A, B, C, A, A, B, B, C, C, A, A, A, B, B, B, C, C, C, until you reach the bottom right corner.

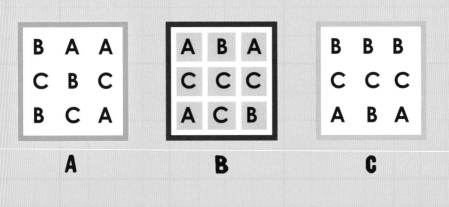

A
```
B A A
C B C
B C A
```

B
```
A B A
C C C
A C B
```

C
```
B B B
C C C
A B A
```

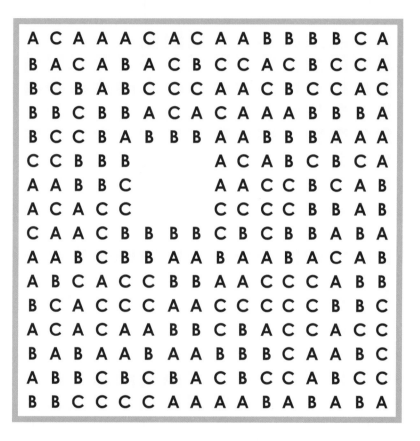

PUZZLE 36
The symbol on the flag reveals a number. What is it?

MY GRAY CELLS ARE JUMPING!

PUZZLE 37

Start at the middle 2 and move from circle to touching circle. Collect three numbers and add them to the 2. How many different routes are there to make a total of 12?

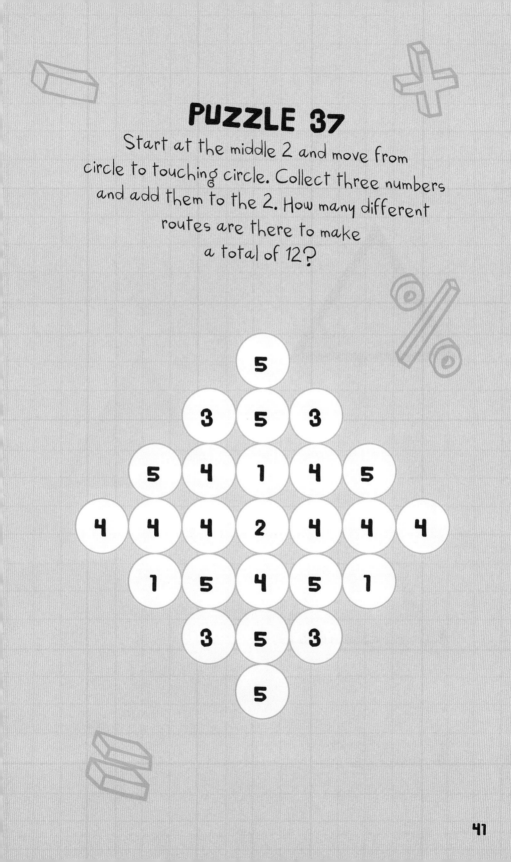

PUZZLE 38

What number should replace
the question mark?

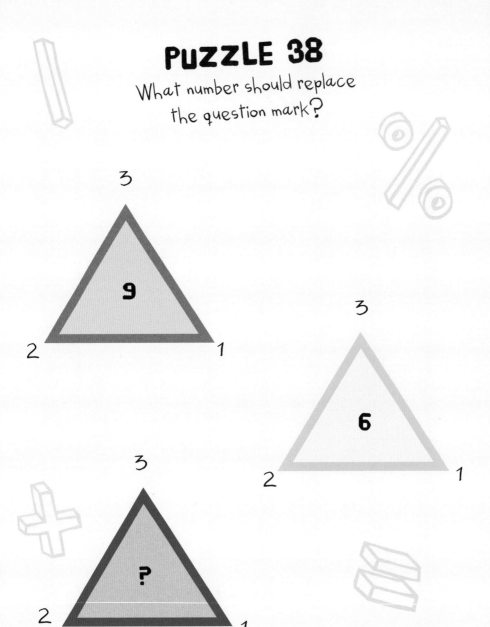

3

9

2   1

3

6

2   1

3

?

2   1

Hint: The numbers inside
each triangle will point you
in the right direction.

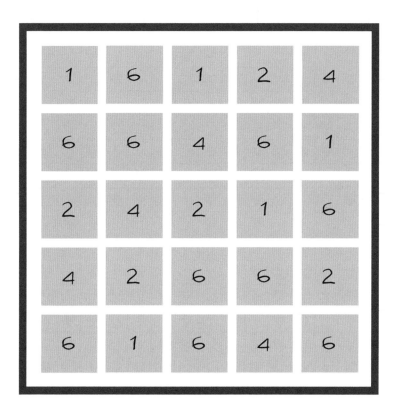

PUZZLE 39
Divide the box using four lines so that each shape adds up to the same total. How is this done?

PUZZLE 40

The symbols in the above grid follow a pattern. Can you figure it out and find the missing section?

PUZZLE 41

Scales 1 and 2 are in perfect balance. If one C is the same as four A's, how many A's are needed to balance the third set?

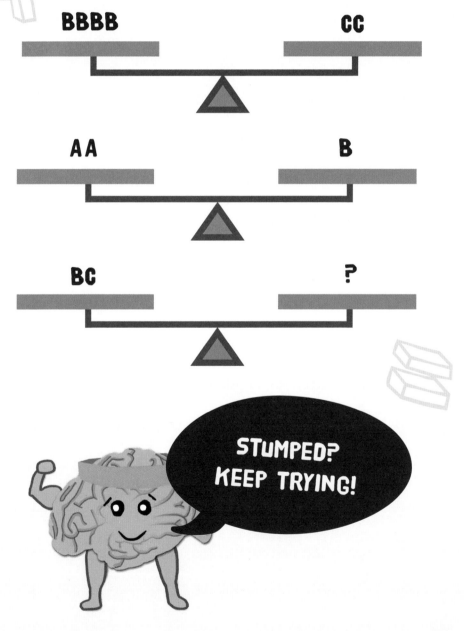

STUMPED? KEEP TRYING!

PUZZLE 42

The missing number in the middle of the star is related to all those in its points. What is the number?

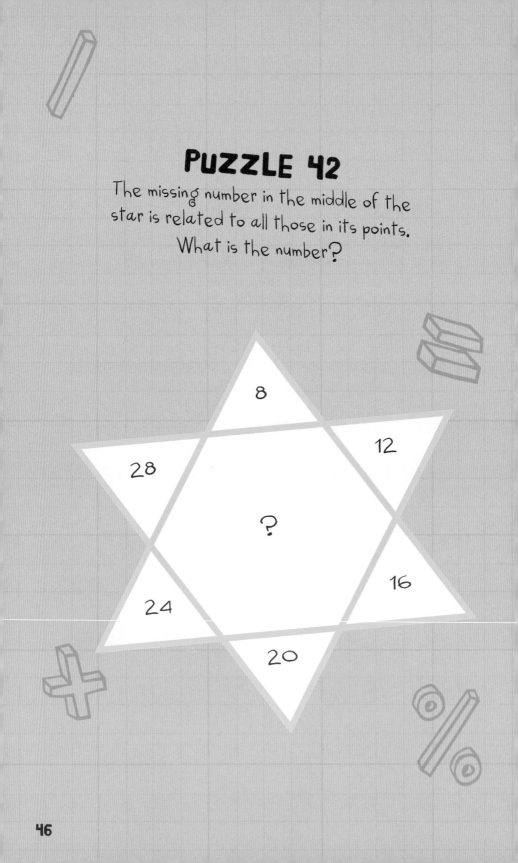

8

12

28

?

24

16

20

PUZZLE 43

How many rectangles of any size can you find in this diagram? Remember a square is also a rectangle!

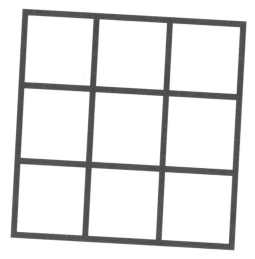

PUZZLE 44

What number should replace the question mark to continue the series?

9   10   11   12

1   5   2   ?   3   7   4   8

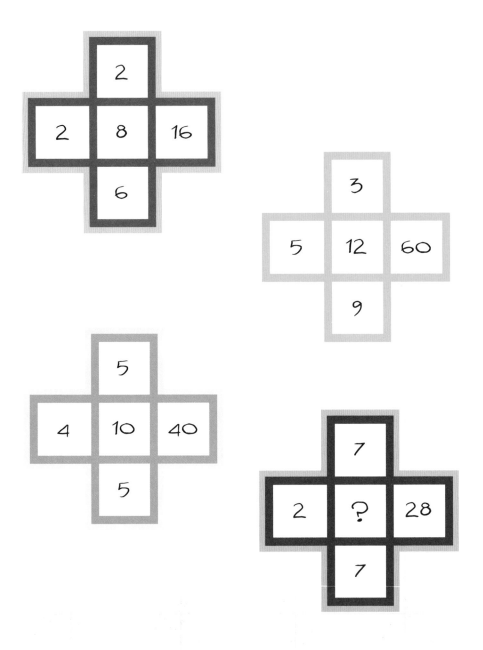

PUZZLE 45

What number should replace the question mark?

PUZZLE 46

Which squares contain the same numbers?

	A	**B**	**C**	**D**
1	2 3 1	1 3 1	2 1 2	1 3 6
2	4 2 4	6 4 5	2 2 2	3 4 2
3	3 3 4	6 3 1	5 6 5	1 1 1
4	3 3 3	2 4 2	3 4 1	5 5 5

PUZZLE 47

What number should replace the question mark? Hint: The answer may not be in the same segment.

I THINK I KNOW THIS ONE.

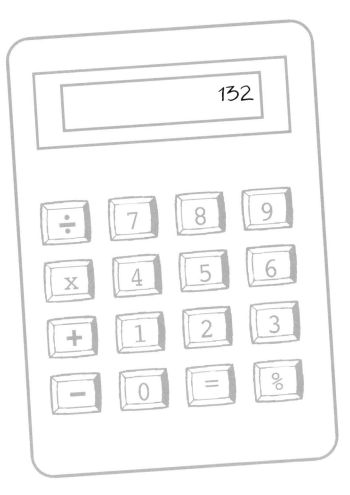

PUZZLE 48

One two-digit number should be used to divide the one shown on the calculator to get the answer 11. What is the number?

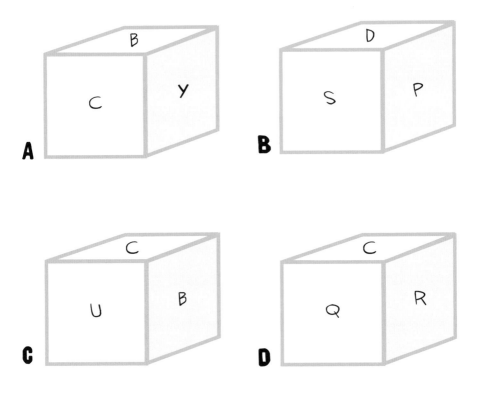

A — B, C, Y

B — D, S, P

C — C, U, B

D — C, Q, R

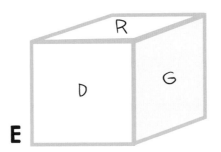

E — R, D, G

PUZZLE 49

Which cube is the odd one out? It helps not to think in straight lines!

PUZZLE 50

Fill in the empty boxes so that every line adds up to the same, including the lines that go from corner to corner. Which two numbers will be used to do this?

3		3	0	3
	3	3	3	
3	3	3	3	3
	3	3	3	
3		3		3

PUZZLE 51

What number should go in the middle?

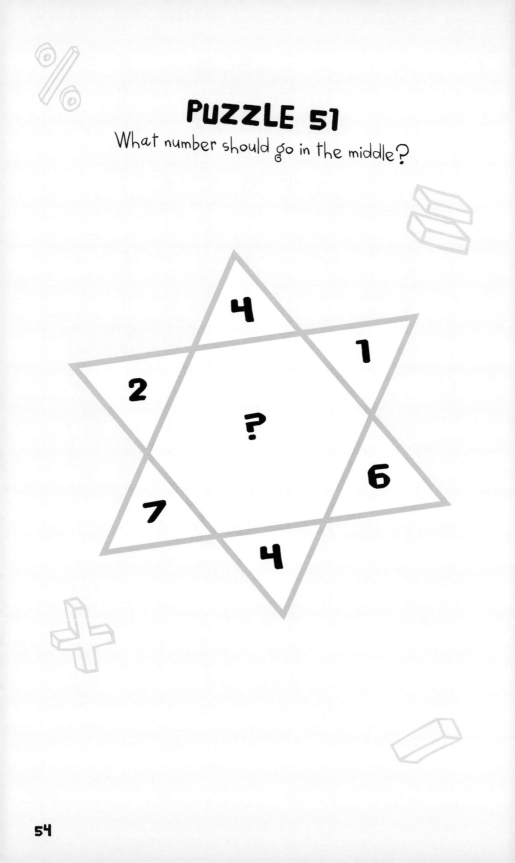

PUZZLE 52

Cut the cake slices out carefully and rearrange them to find the age. How old was the birthday boy?

PuZZLE 53

Which letter is needed to replace
the question mark? Is it F, S,
or B?

PUZZLE 54

Zap the spaceship by finding a one-digit number which will divide without remainder all the numbers which appear on it. What number should you use?

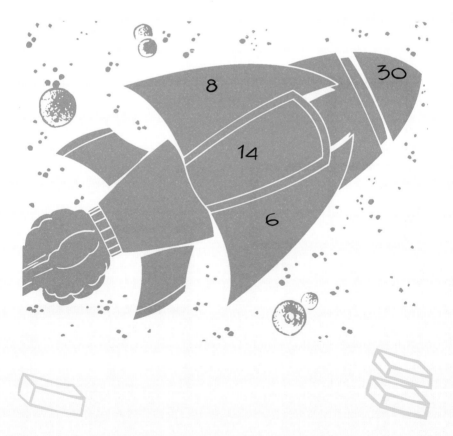

PUZZLE 55

What is the missing number?

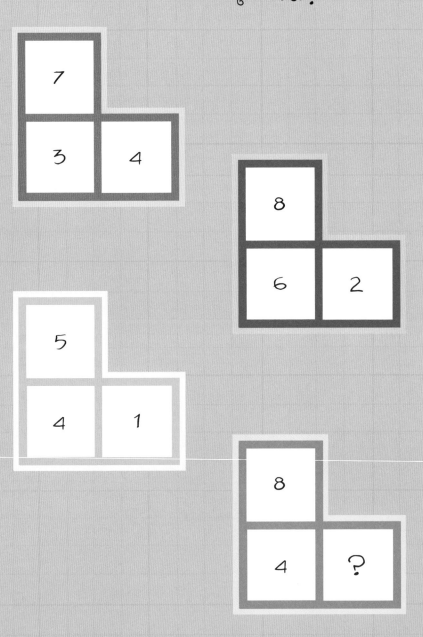

PUZZLE 56

Here is a series of numbers. What number should replace the question mark?

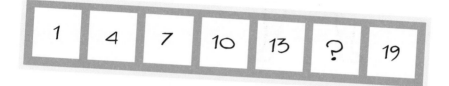

| 1 | 4 | 7 | 10 | 13 | ? | 19 |

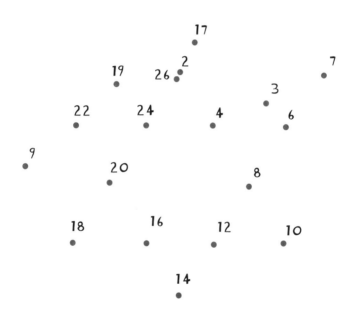

PUZZLE 57

Connect the dots using even numbers only. Start at the lowest and discover the object. What is it?

PUZZLE 58

Which cube is the odd one out?

PUZZLE 59

How many 4's can be found in this Stegosaurus?

PUZZLE 60
What number is missing from the final box?

	1	2	3	4
A	9	15	9	1
B	6	11	3	13
C	4	5	2	12
D	7	5	1	8

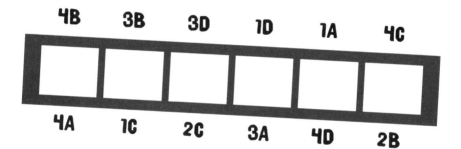

4B   3B   3D   1D   1A   4C

4A   1C   2C   3A   4D   2B

PUZZLE 61

Find the correct six numbers to put in the frame.
There are two choices for each square, for example
1A would give the number 9. When the correct
numbers have been found, an easy series will appear.
What is the series?

PUZZLE 62

Find a number to replace the question mark.

I'M GETTING INTO THE SWING OF THIS!

PUZZLE 63

Which of the numbers in the square is the
odd one out and why?

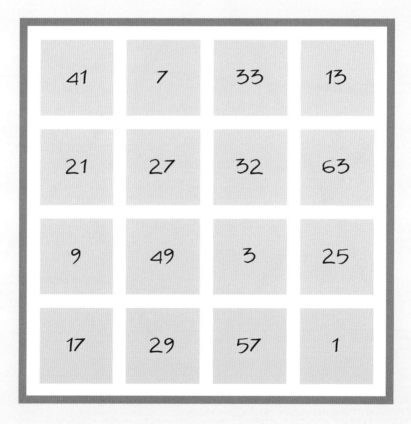

41	7	33	13
21	27	32	63
9	49	3	25
17	29	57	1

PUZZLE 64

The missing number in the star is related to all those in its points. What is it?

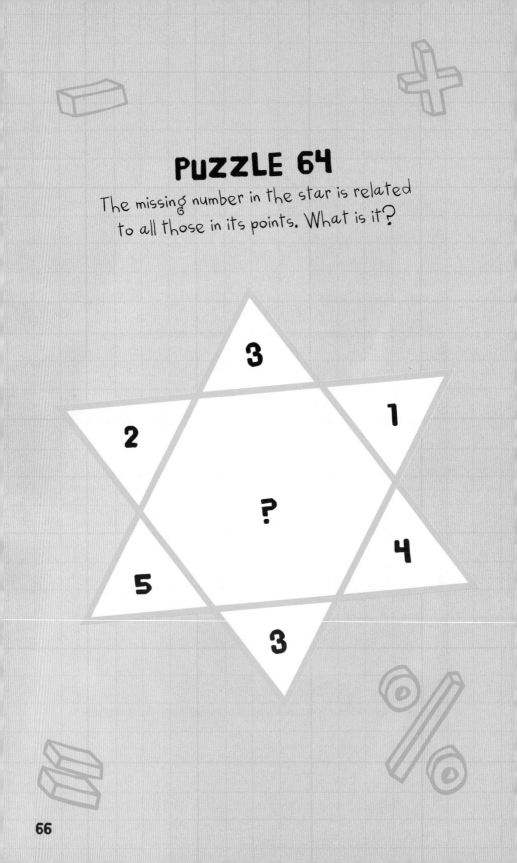

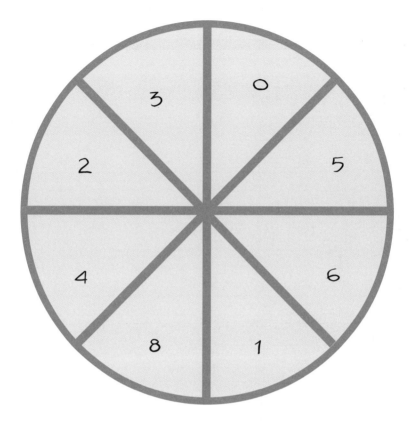

PUZZLE 65

Each slice of this cake has a number written on it. Using the numbers shown, how many different ways are there to add three numbers together to make a total of 13? A number can be used more than once, but a group cannot be repeated in a different order.

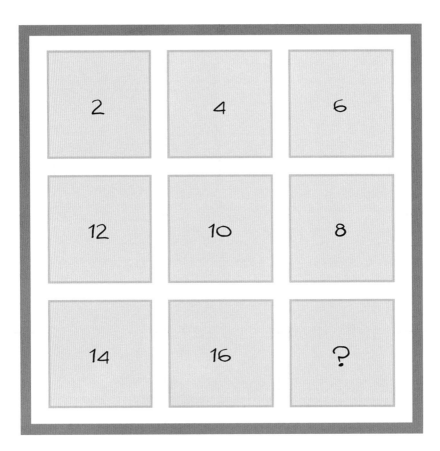

2	4	6
12	10	8
14	16	?

PUZZLE 66
Complete the numbers in the square.

PUZZLE 67

Which of these pictures is not of the same box?

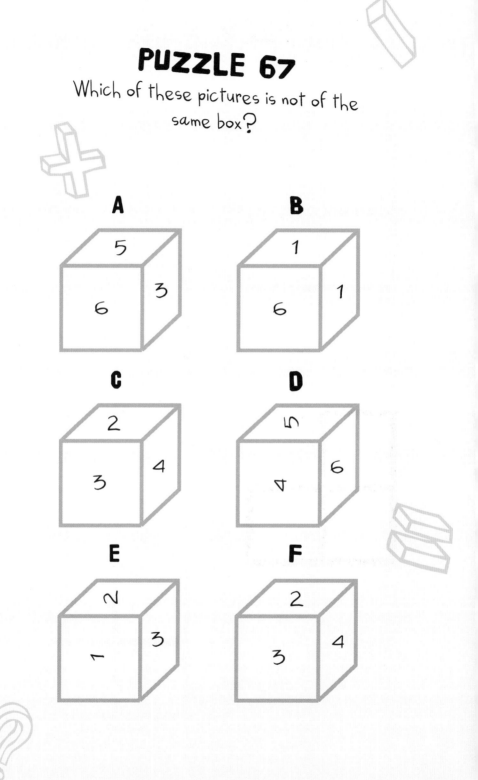

A

5
6
3

B

1
6
1

C

2
3
4

D

5
4
6

E

2
1
3

F

2
3
4

PUZZLE 68

What number is missing from the box?

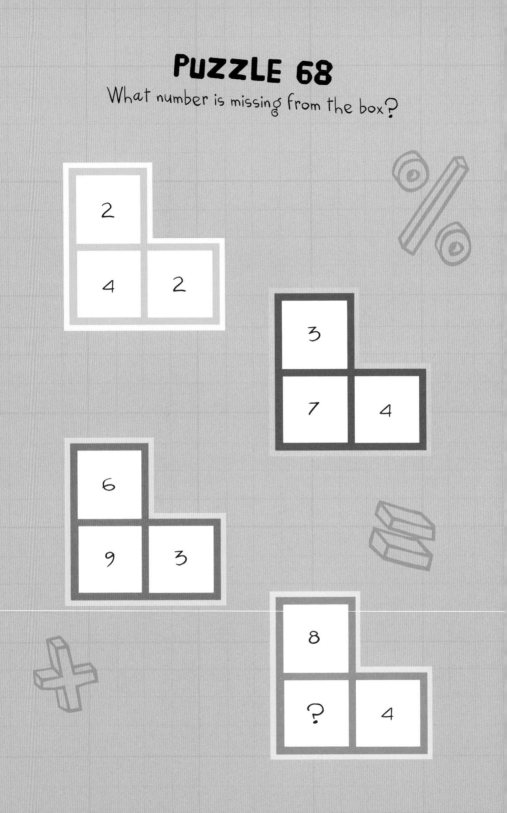

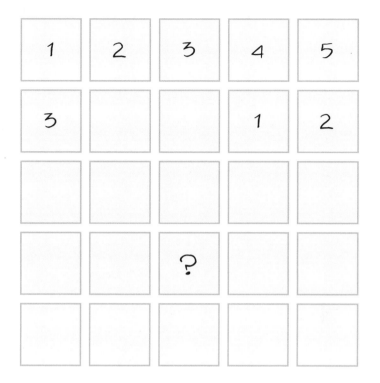

PUZZLE 69

Fill up this square with the numbers 1 to 5 so that no row, column, or diagonal line of five squares uses the same number more than once. What number should replace the question mark?

CAN YOUR MOM DO THIS ONE?

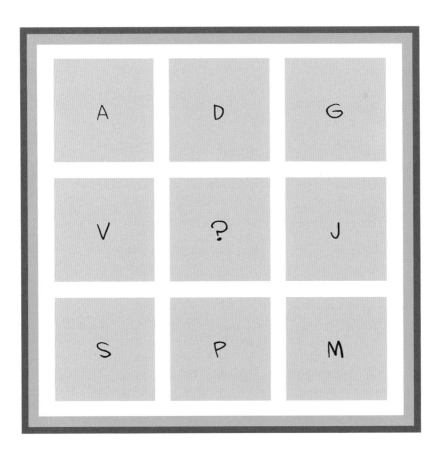

PUZZLE 70
Find the missing letter. Is it Y, D, or J?

PUZZLE 71

Move up or across from the bottom left-hand 5 to the top right-hand 5. Collect nine numbers and add them together. What is the highest you can score?

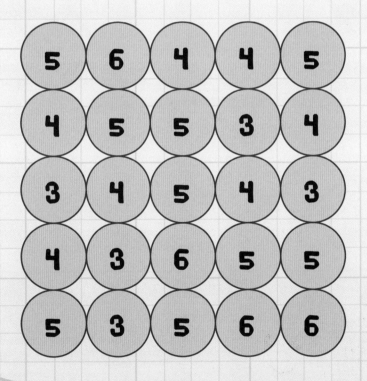

PUZZLE 72

What number is needed to replace the question mark?

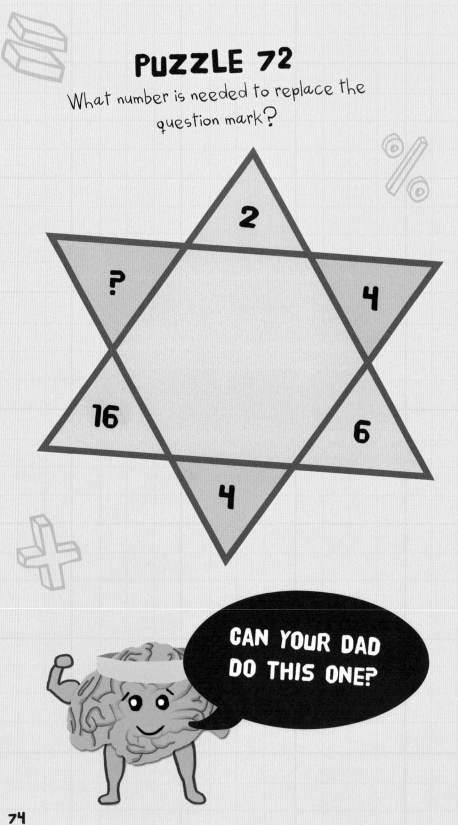

8	4	4
3	1	2
7	2	5
6	5	1
9	?	3

PUZZLE 73

The numbers in the middle section have some connection with those down the sides. Find out what it is and tell us what should replace the question mark.

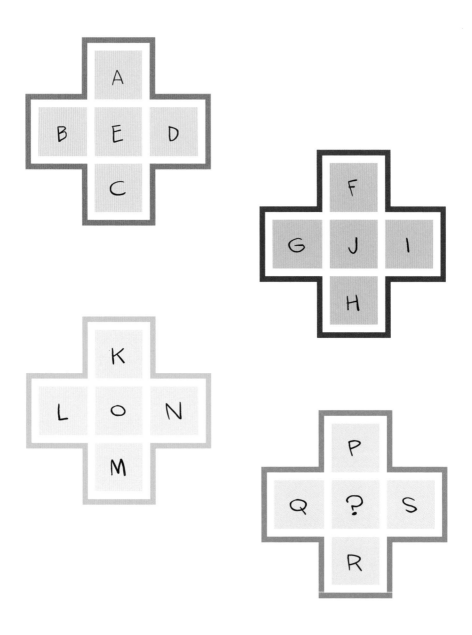

PUZZLE 74

What letter is needed to complete the final cross? Is it B, T, or K?

PUZZLE 75

Move up or across from the bottom
left-hand 2 to the top right-hand 3. Collect
nine numbers and add them together.
What is the highest you can score?

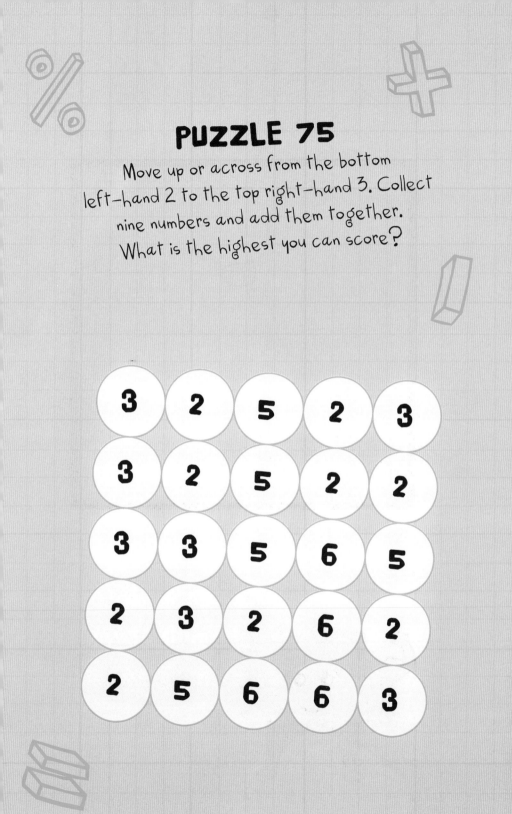

PUZZLE 76

What number completes the square?

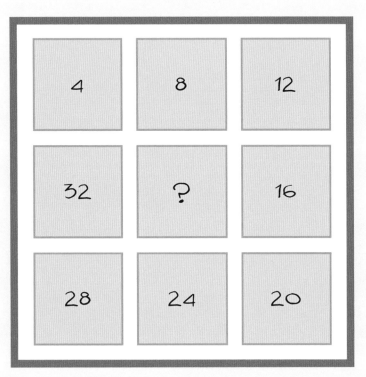

4	8	12
32	?	16
28	24	20

UP AND AT 'EM!

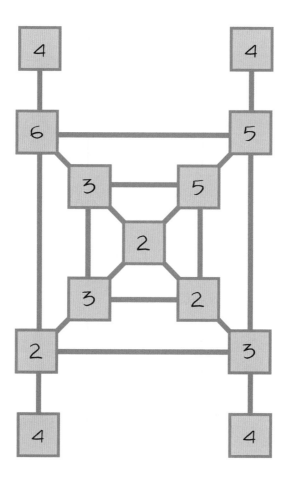

PUZZLE 77

Start at any corner and follow the lines. Add up the first four numbers you meet and then add on the corner number. What is the highest you can score?

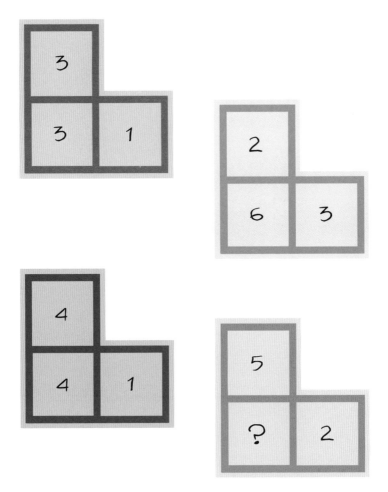

PUZZLE 78

Find a number to replace the question mark.

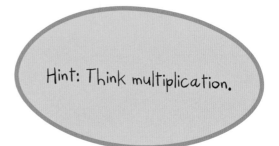

Hint: Think multiplication.

PUZZLE 79

Place in the middle box a number larger than 1.
If the number is the correct one,
all the other numbers can be divided
by it without leaving any remainder.
What is the number?

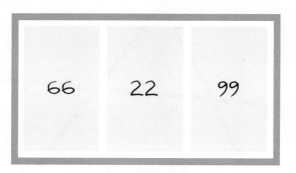

66   22   99

?

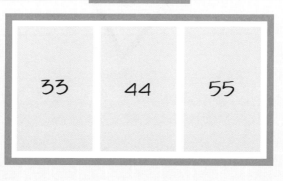

33   44   55

PUZZLE 80

Complete the star by replacing the question mark with a letter.

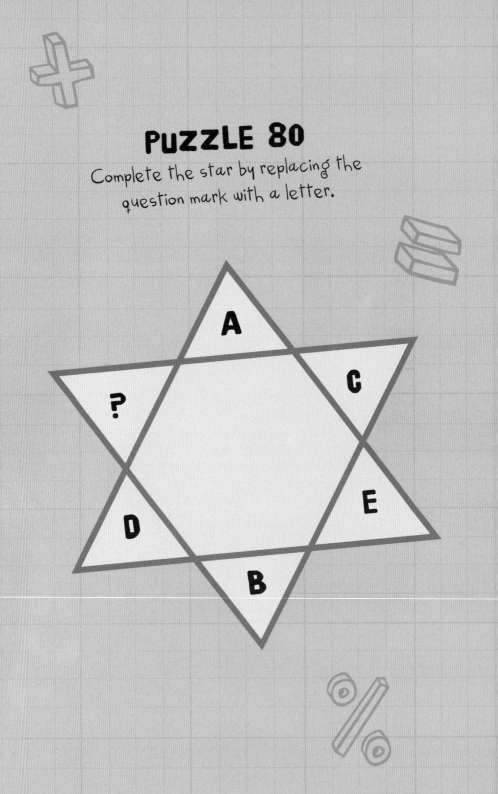

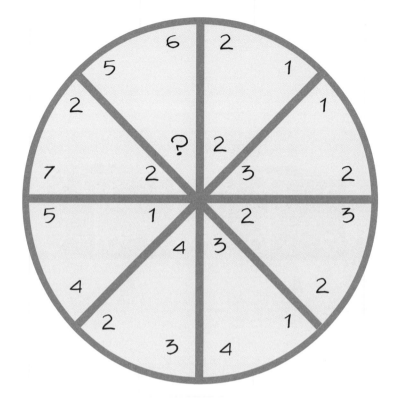

PUZZLE 81

Each sector of the circle follows a
pattern. What number should replace
the question mark?

LIMBERING UP!

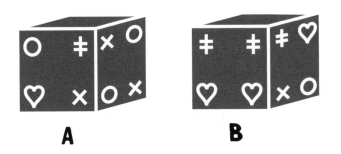

PUZZLE 82

Which of these cubes is the odd one out?

PUZZLE 83

Here is an unusual safe. Each of the buttons must be pressed only once in the correct order to open it. The last button is marked F. The number of moves and the direction is marked on each button. Thus, 1i would mean one move in, while 1o would mean one move out. 1c would mean one move clockwise and 1a would mean one move counterclockwise. Which button is the first you must press?

Here's a clue: look around the outer rim.

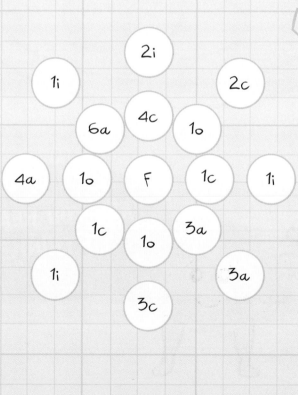

PUZZLE 84

If you look carefully, you should see why the numbers are written as they are. What number should replace the question mark?

ARE YOU READY TO THINK?

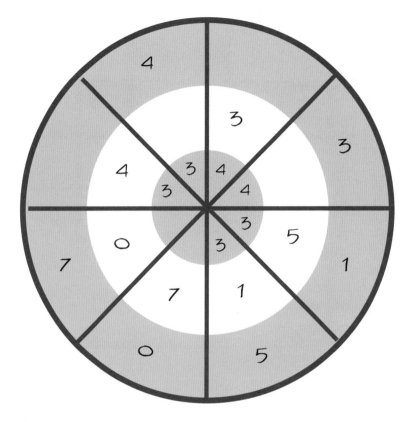

PUZZLE 85

Each slice of this cake adds up to the same number. Also, each ring of the cake totals the same. What number should appear in the blanks?

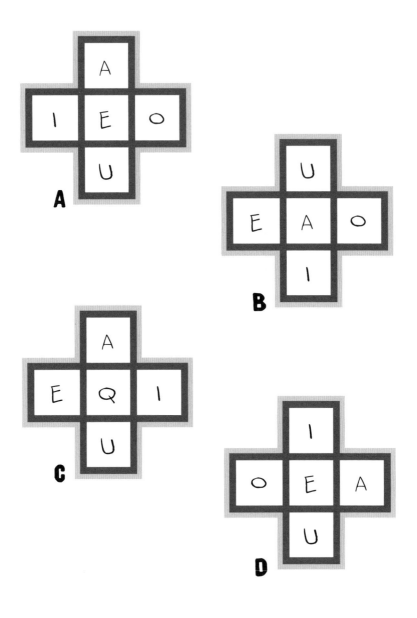

PUZZLE 86

Which of these crosses is the odd one out?

PUZZLE 87

Cut the cake slices out carefully and rearrange them to find the age. How old was the birthday boy?

PUZZLE 88

The first two sets of scales are in balance. Which symbol is needed to balance the third set?

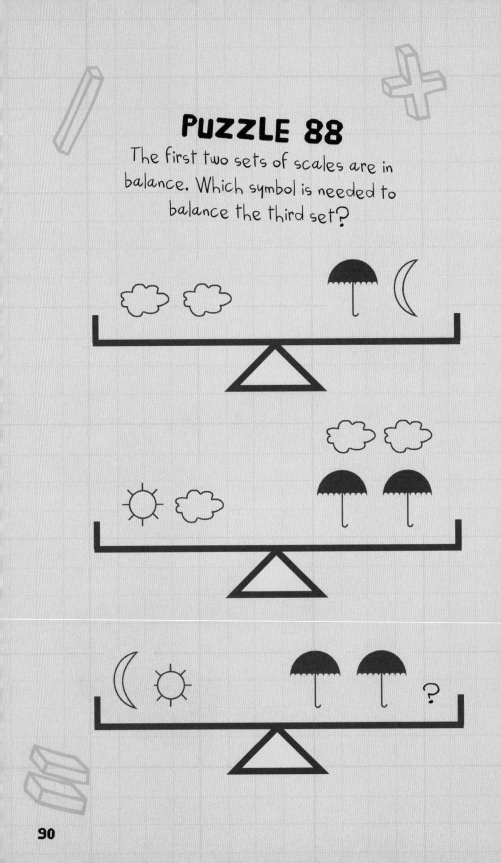

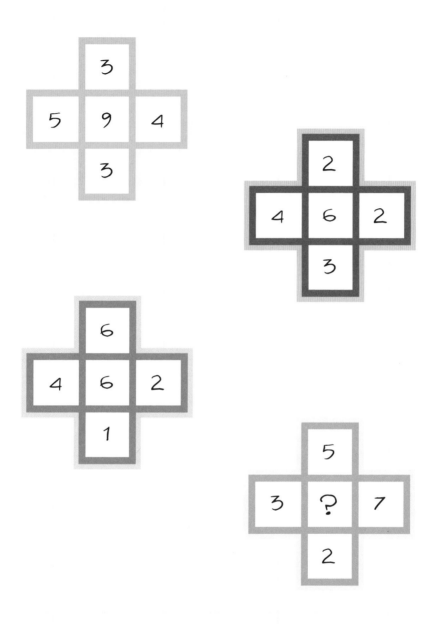

PUZZLE 89

Find a number to complete the last cross.

ANSWERS

ANSWER 1
Two-ninths.

ANSWER 2
A = 8, B = 2.

ANSWER 3
15.

ANSWER 4
C. The symbols repeat in the sequence + − × ÷, which zigzags back and forth across the rows of the grid.

ANSWER 5
23.

ANSWER 6
5.

ANSWER 7
10.

ANSWER 8
2. The numbers in each sector total 12.

ANSWER 9
36.

ANSWER 10
5.

ANSWER 11
3. The numbers all increase by two if you start at the top left and work clockwise.

ANSWER 12
3. The number is found in 3 overlapping shapes.

ANSWER 13
5. The number at the top of each triangle equals the total of the numbers at the base.

ANSWER 14
8 in the outer section at the top, 3 in the outer section below, and 5 in the inner one.

ANSWER 15
16. The number in the middle of each square equals the sum of the numbers around the outside.

ANSWER 16
25, in the fourth column.

ANSWER 17
W.

ANSWER 18
45 minutes.

ANSWER 19
4. The total of each horizontal line increases by 1.

ANSWER 20
2. In each sector, subtract the smaller of the outside numbers from the larger and put the remainder in the middle.

ANSWER 21
17 of 1V, 2V, 5V, and 10V coins.

ANSWER 22
52.

ANSWER 23
10.

ANSWER 24
Large hand on 4, small hand on 5. The hands advance by one at each turn.

ANSWER 25
7. Add together A, B, and C to get D.

ANSWER 26
E. The other four cubes have one of each symbol on both sides.

ANSWER 27
20.

ANSWER 28
54. The digits are reversed at each turn.

ANSWER 29
22.

ANSWER 30
1. In each row the values of the alphabetic position of the left and middle letters are added together and the answer, written as a letter, is put in the right column.

ANSWER 31
3.

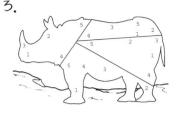

ANSWER 32
Divide, plus, and plus.

ANSWER 33
R. The letters, reading backward from Z in alphabetical order, go in continuous vertical lines.

ANSWER 34
16.

ANSWER 35
A.

ANSWER 36
4. A 4 and its mirror image are placed together.

ANSWER 37
6.

ANSWER 38
3. The numbers from the top of the triangles are added and put in the middle of the first triangle; the numbers from the left corners of the triangles are added and put in the middle of the second triangle; and the numbers from the right corners of the triangles are added and put in the middle of the third triangle.

ANSWER 39

1	6	1	2	4
6	6	4	6	1
2	4	2	1	6
4	2	6	6	2
6	1	6	4	6

ANSWER 40
Start at the top right corner and work in an inward spiral. The pattern is: two ticks, one heart, two faces, one tick, two hearts, one face, etc.

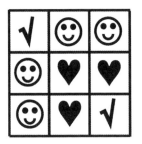

ANSWER 41
6.

ANSWER 42
4. All the numbers are multiples of 4.

ANSWER 43
36.

ANSWER 44
6. Move from triangle to triangle, beginning on the left, to read 1, 2, 3, 4. Start again to get 5, 6, 7, 8. Then move to the top to get 9, 10, 11, 12.

ANSWER 45
14. The numbers at the top and bottom are added together, and the number on the right is divided by the number on the left. The answer to both sums is the same, and it goes in the middle of the cross.

ANSWER 46
3B and 1D.

ANSWER 47
40. The numbers on the outside of each segment are multiplied together, and the answer is put on the inside of the diagonally opposite sector.

ANSWER 48
12.

ANSWER 49
A. It is the only one which contains a letter with no curves (Y).

ANSWER 50
O and 6.

ANSWER 51
8. The values in opposite points all add up to 8.

ANSWER 52
21.

ANSWER 53
B. Starting from the top left corner, go down and up in a continuous zigzag. Jump back three letters each time.

ANSWER 54
2.

ANSWER 55
4. Subtract the bottom number from the top and put the difference in the box on the right.

ANSWER 56
16. The numbers increase by 3 each time.

ANSWER 57
A star.

ANSWER 58
3. It is the only one with a round letter (O) on one face.

ANSWER 59
30.

ANSWER 60
2. Add the lower numbers and place the answer on top.

ANSWER 61
1 3 5 7 9 11. The numbers increase by 2 each time.

ANSWER 62
14. The numbers on the outer rim subtract to give the inner numbers in each segment.

ANSWER 63
32. It is the only even number.

ANSWER 64
6. Add opposite pairs of numbers. All totals add up to 6.

ANSWER 65
8.

ANSWER 66
18. A simple arithmetical progression increasing by 2 at each step.

ANSWER 67
B.

ANSWER 68
12. Add the number at the top and the number at bottom right and put the answer at bottom left.

ANSWER 69
4.

ANSWER 70
Y. Start from the top left corner and work in a clockwise spiral, skipping two letters of the alphabet each time.

ANSWER 71
42.

ANSWER 72
36. Reading clockwise from the top, the first three numbers are squared and the answers are placed in the point diagonally opposite.

ANSWER 73
6. The number down the right-hand side is taken from the number down the left-hand side to give the number in the middle section.

ANSWER 74
T. The alphabet is written in the crosses in a spiral.

ANSWER 75
41.

ANSWER 76
36. Starting from the top left the numbers increase by 4 in a clockwise spiral.

ANSWER 77
23.

ANSWER 78
10. Multiply the top and bottom right numbers. Put the answer at the bottom left.

ANSWER 79
11.

ANSWER 80
F. The letters form pairs that are consecutive in the alphabet. The members of each pair are put in opposite points. F is the 6th letter.

ANSWER 81
1. Each sector's total increases by 1.

ANSWER 82
D. It is the only cube which does not have a face with two pairs of identical symbols.

ANSWER 83
1i, found between 4a and 3c.

ANSWER 84
3. The number is found in 3 overlapping shapes.

ANSWER 85
2.

ANSWER 86
C. All the others contain only vowels. C has a Q in it.

ANSWER 87
5.

ANSWER 88
One sun. The values are: Cloud = 3; Umbrella = 2; Moon = 4; Sun = 7.

ANSWER 89
10. The numbers at the left and right are added together and the numbers at the top and bottom are multiplied. The answer to both sums is the same, and it goes in the middle of the cross.